Learning Tree
1 2 3

Bees

By Hannah E. Glease
Illustrated by Mike Atkinson

CHERRYTREE BOOKS

Read this book and see if you can answer the questions. Ask an adult or an older friend to tell you if your answers are right or to help you if you find the questions difficult. Often there is more than one answer to a question.

Never try to pick up a bee. You will frighten it and it may sting you.

A Cherrytree Book

Designed and produced by
A S Publishing

First published 1991
by Cherrytree Press Ltd
a subsidiary of
The Chivers Company Ltd
Windsor Bridge Road
Bath, Avon BA2 3AX

Copyright © Cherrytree Press Ltd 1991

British Library Cataloguing in Publication Data
Glease, Hannah E.
  Bees
  1. Bees
  I. Title   II. Atkinson, Michael   III. Series
  595.799

  ISBN 0-7451-5154-X

Printed and bound in Italy by L.E.G.O. s.p.a., Vicenza

This is a bumblebee.
It is feeding on the flowers.

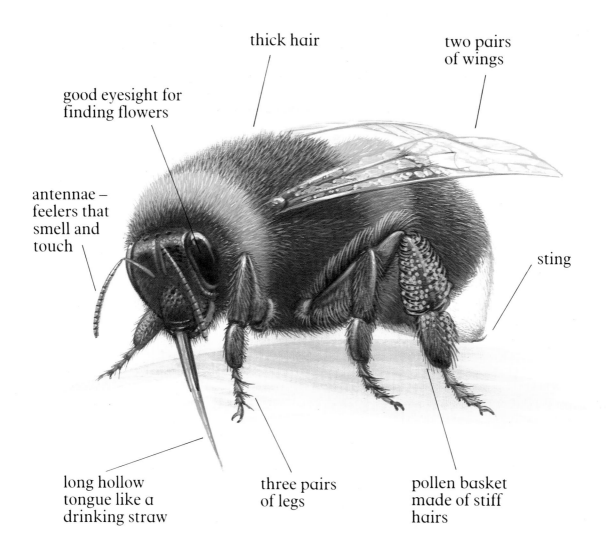

good eyesight for finding flowers

thick hair

two pairs of wings

antennae – feelers that smell and touch

sting

long hollow tongue like a drinking straw

three pairs of legs

pollen basket made of stiff hairs

Bees are insects.
They have six legs and two pairs of wings.

A bumblebee has a long
hollow tongue.
It uses it to suck up the sweet
nectar from flowers.
It makes the nectar into
honey.

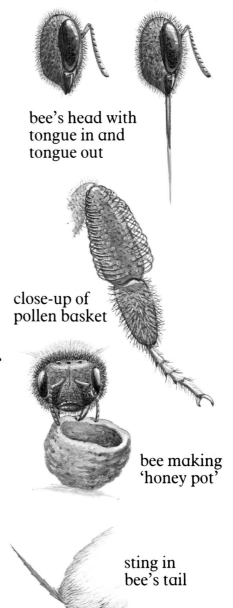

bee's head with
tongue in and
tongue out

It also eats pollen.
It carries some pollen home in
'baskets' on its back legs.

close-up of
pollen basket

The bee makes wax in its body.
It uses the wax in its nest.
It covers its eggs with wax and
makes 'pots' for honey.

bee making
'honey pot'

Bees have a sting to protect
themselves.
They will not sting you unless
you annoy them.

sting in
bee's tail

This is a queen bee.
In winter she sleeps in a tiny hole under the
ground.

In spring she wakes.
She drinks lots of nectar to make her strong.
Then she finds a place to make a new nest.

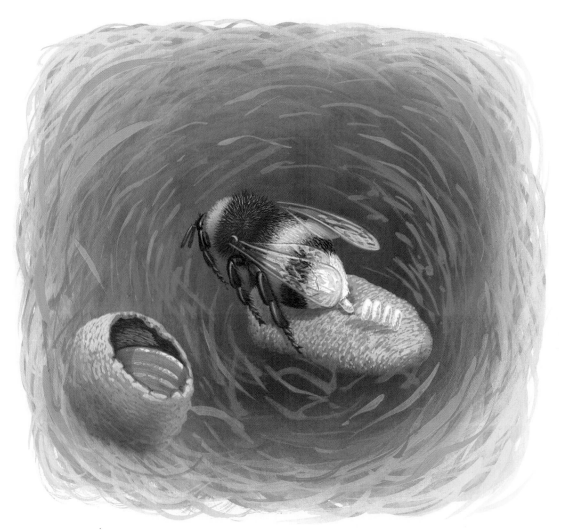

Inside her nest the queen makes a wax 'pot'.
She fills it with a store of nectar.
Then she makes a soft cushion of pollen.

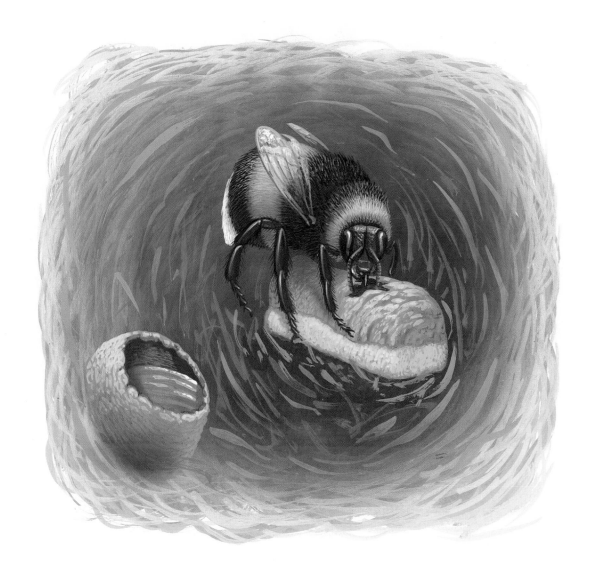

She lays her eggs on the cushion.
She covers the eggs with wax to protect them.

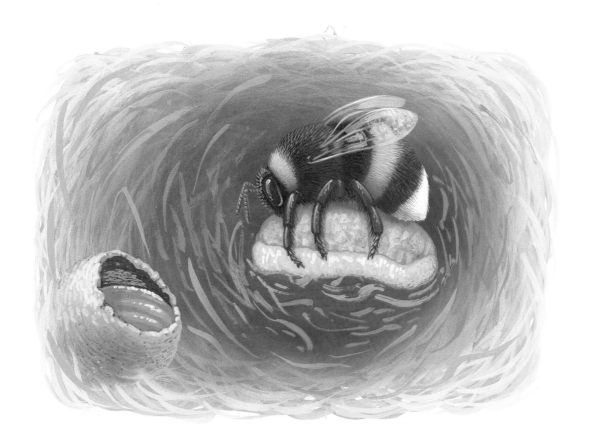

The queen settles down on top of her eggs to keep them warm.
She feeds on nectar from her pot when bad weather stops her going out.

The eggs hatch into grubs.

The queen feeds the grubs nectar and pollen.
They grow bigger and bigger.

Then they spin a silky coat round themselves.
It is called a cocoon.

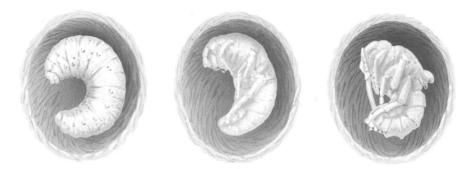

Inside their cocoons, the grubs slowly change into bees.

The queen lays more eggs. She is always busy.

The new bees are all females.
They are smaller than their mother but they
work as hard.
They are called worker bees.

Every day the workers collect pollen and
nectar for the new grubs in the nest.
The queen lays more and more eggs.

workers

drone

new
queen

At the end of summer some new queen bees hatch.
A few male bees hatch too.
They are called drones. They do no work.
They fly from the nest with the new queens.

15

The male bees mate with the new queens.
That is their only job.

The workers and drones do not live long.
Most die after about four weeks.

Only the new queen bees are strong enough to live through the winter.

They find a warm hiding place and sleep until spring.

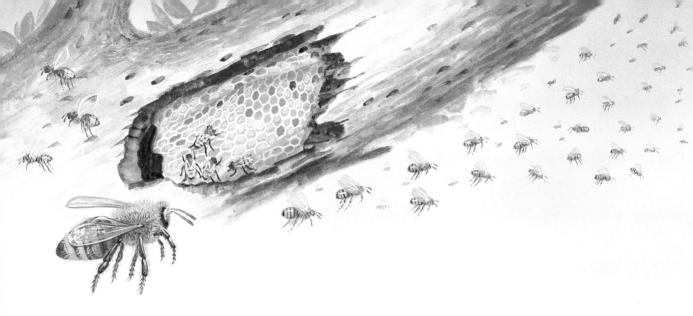

Bumblebees are not the only kind of bee.
Honeybees live in even bigger nests.

People keep honeybees in wooden hives.
We eat the honey that they make.

Inside their hives, honeybees
make wax honeycombs. We
eat the honey from them.

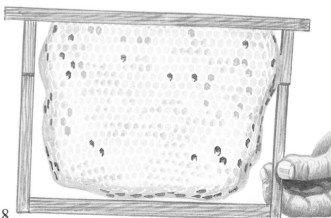

18

Some bees live on their own.
The mother bee lays one egg at a time and leaves it.
She leaves a store of honey and pollen for when the egg hatches.

Carpenter bees make nests in old wood. They have strong jaws to chew the wood.

Leafcutter bees cut bits of leaves from plants. They stick them together to make a nest.

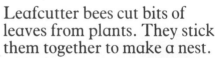
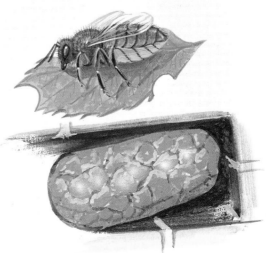

Mining bees make nests in the ground. They pile up the soil.

Bees protect themselves with their stings.
But some of their enemies are too big.
Bears and badgers attack bees' nests.
They love to eat the grubs and honey.
The bees cannot sting through their fur.

Hornets eat bees and
their grubs.
Their skin is too hard
for a sting to pierce.

hornet

20

More about bees

Kinds of bee
Some bees are social. They live together in large nests called colonies. Sometimes they fly together in a swarm. Other bees live on their own. They are called solitary bees.

Bees and flowers
When bees and other insects visit flowers they help the flowers. They carry pollen from one to another. A flower cannot make seeds unless it has pollen from another flower.

When a honeybee finds lots of flowers, it tells the other bees in its hive. It does a dance over the honeycomb. The dance lets the other bees know where the flowers are.

Bees always take the most direct route back to their nest. They make a beeline for it.

Working wings
The buzzing noise that makes bees sound so busy is made by their wings as they fly. Bees also use their wings as fans. They fan cool fresh air into their nests and hot stale air out.

Sting in the tail
Bees defend their nests by stinging their enemies. The sting is a pointed tube through which the bee squirts poison. Bumblebees can sting more than once. A honeybee can sting only once. Its sting has barbs that stick in its enemy's flesh. The bee flies off without it, and dies.

Enemies
Lots of animals like to eat bees. Other insects are the bees' most dangerous enemies. The wax moth lays its eggs in bees' nests. The grubs feed on the wax cells and the bee grubs die. The cuckoo bee is like a cuckoo bird. It lays its eggs in other bees' nests. The bees from the nest bring up its babies.

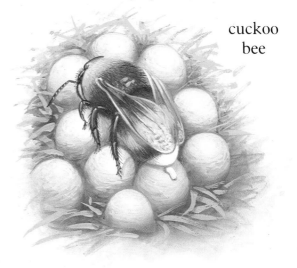

cuckoo bee

1

1 What do bees eat?

2 What is a mother bee called?

3 Draw a bee on a flower.

4 Why do bees like flowers?

5 How many legs has a bee?

6 Are worker bees male or female?

7 Is a drone male or female?

8 What happens to queen bees during the winter?

9 How much work do drones do?

10 What do bees make that we can eat?

2

11 What is the queen bee's job?

12 What do worker bees do?

13 What do bee eggs turn into before they become bees?

14 What kind of bee mates with a queen?

15 Why do flowers need bees?

16 How does a bee carry pollen back to its nest?

17 What happens to worker bees at the end of the summer?

18 These are bumblebees. One is a queen, one is a worker, one is a drone? Which do you see most often? Why?

queen

drone

worker

3

19 During the spring and summer, watch bees at work. You may see a queen bee on sunny days in spring. Keep a notebook and write down what flowers you find bees on. Which flowers do they like best? Make a note of the time of day. Is it sunny or cloudy?

20 Look out for different kinds of bees. Remember their colours and shapes. Look in an insect guide book to find out their names.

21 What is a cocoon?

22 How do honeybees tell the other bees in their hive where they have found new flowers?

23 Can you name two kinds of solitary bee?

24 The queen bee stores nectar in a pot. What is the pot made of?

25 A hornet is a kind of wasp that attacks bees. The outside of a hornet's body is very hard. How does this help it?

26 Where does a carpenter bee make its nest?

27 Where does a miner bee make its nest?

28 What kind of bee makes a nest with leaves?

29 Why is a cuckoo bee like a cuckoo bird?

30 Look at a picture of a honeycomb. The cells the bees make have six sides. They are hexagonal. Draw a pattern of hexagonal shapes like a honeycomb.

31 Why should we take care never to harm a bee?

Index